Copyright © 1986 Beverley Parkin

Published by
Lion Publishing plc
Icknield Way, Tring, Herts, England
ISBN 0 85648 905 0
Lion Publishing Corporation
10885 Textile Road, Belleville, Michigan 48111, USA
ISBN 0 85648 905 0
Albatross Books Pty Ltd
PO Box 320, Sutherland, NSW 2232, Australia
ISBN 0 86760 646 0

First edition 1986

Bible quotations from *The Holy Bible,*
New International Version: copyright©
New York International Bible Society, 1978

Acknowledgments
Cover photograph by Picturebank
Illustrations by Sandra Littleton Evans
Text photographs by S. & O. Mathews
with additional photographs by
Alan Beaumont, Wallflowers, Holly;
John Feltwell, Fuschias; Sonia Halliday Photographs:
F.H.C. Birch, Gladiolus, Sonia Halliday, Violets;
Lion Publishing: David Alexander, endpapers,
Gentian, Heart's-ease Pansies;
Sutton Seeds, Torquay, Carnations

British Library Cataloguing in Publication Data
Parkin, Beverley
   Flowers with love.
   1. Christian life
   I. Title
   248.4   BV4501.2
   ISBN 0 85648 905 0

Printed and bound in Italy

Flowers with love

BEVERLEY PARKIN

A LION BOOK

Tring · Belleville · Sydney

Tulips

Tulips are gregarious flowers. They are at their best en-masse, great companies of them filling flower-beds, dressed in different coloured uniforms, heads up, leaves swinging. There are fantastic displays of massed tulips at the Kirkennof Gardens in Holland and in springtime people flock to see them.

One of my favourites is the parrot tulip, ragged green and cream, or green and red striped petals, weird and waxy. When I was training at the Constance Spry flower school, a street trader always kept a bunch of these parrot tulips to give me on Fridays, lovely man!

After cutting or buying tulips, cut off the white stem-ends, remove any paper and soak in deep water overnight. I like to use tulips in a free display, cutting them to different heights. Placed near a window and turned a fraction every day, the stems will twist and turn, seeking the source of light.

There are times in our lives when we desperately seek for a solution to a problem, twisting and turning, spending sleepless nights, exhausted by nervous strain. But if, like the tulips, we seek the light for a way through our problems we shall find real relief from our anxieties.

> **66** Jesus said, 'I am the light of the world. Whoever follows me will never walk in darkness, but will have the light of life. **99**
> FROM JOHN'S GOSPEL, CHAPTER 8

Arrange tulips in an oasis-filled low bowl, place driftwood in front and arrange large leaves around the base.

Gladiolus

The regal queen of flowers, the gladiolus, presides over the herbaceous border surveying her lesser subjects. The varied shapes and colours give a wide selection for cutting, although I prefer to buy commercially grown flowers, rather than rob the garden!

Gladioli have the spiky shape ideal for an arrangement outline, providing a strong background for other flowers. Pinch out the top bud to encourage the lower buds to open fully.

I place the first gladiolus in position in a triangle arrangement and then insert the other stems so that they angle in towards the first bloom. This centre flower is the guide for all the other blooms and foliage.

We all have our pride, and we like to depend on our own resources. But Jesus asks for the central position in our lives. He is our guide and example and we shall not go far wrong if all our thoughts and actions are referred to him.

> **❝** Trust in the Lord with all your heart and lean not on your own understanding; in all your ways acknowledge him, and he will make your paths straight. **❞**
> FROM PROVERBS, CHAPTER 3

Use gladioli as an outline, filling the middle with round blooms and various foliages.

Thrift

After all the storms of winter in Scotland it seems miraculous that the cliffs are so soon covered with a cloak of pink flowers. The little clumps of thrift or sea pinks cling tenaciously to nooks and crannies over the cliff face. Defying the salt spray, they welcome in the spring.

I find yellow and silver lichen, primroses, violets, bluebells and spurge nestling in pockets of soil under sheltering rocks. The sound of the waves dashing below, smoothing and shaping the base of the cliff, seems to echo the creative and universal power of God. The north winds threaten to tear out the little plants yet they thrive and blossom despite the elements.

Jesus never promised us that life would be easy. The sun shines on the good and the bad and the rain refreshes both. But God has a special purpose for each of our lives — however long or short — and he will give us strength and the ability to withstand hardships as we trust him.

> 66 Everyone who hears these words of mine and puts them into practice is like a wise man who built his house on the rock. The rain came down, the streams rose, and the winds blew and beat against that house; yet it did not fall, because it had its foundation on the rock. 99
>
> FROM MATTHEW'S GOSPEL, CHAPTER 7

Take pieces of twisted driftwood, or dry seaweed stems, and arrange them on a pin-holder in a shallow water-filled dish. A few stems of thrift surrounded by pebbles placed at the foot of the branch creates a delicate seaside arrangement.

Gentian

Several years ago my husband and I had the opportunity of visiting Switzerland. It was a special holiday and, most unusually, we were without the children. We meandered through tiny flower-filled villages and drove through majestic mountain passes.

I badly wanted to find gentians growing in the high pastures, or even to pluck an edelweiss from the rocky heights but, alas, it was too late in the year for such delights. Nonetheless, the glory of the snow-capped mountain peaks bathed in a pink alpine glow remains with me.

Driving on a remote road we were halted by a herd of cows. Their different-sized collar bells tinkled and clanged as they swayed past us, and the surrounding rocks reverberated with melodic notes.

Thanks to my bad navigation we once found ourselves on a very narrow track, with the car wheel inches away from a sheer precipice — and I had to walk ahead to guide an understandably reluctant driver. We negotiated it safely, but I had to admit that I really had not looked closely at the map.

This little incident made me realize how easy it is to lose our way in ordinary daily living. There are so many grey areas, situations in which it is difficult to know how to act. It's at times like this that I am especially glad of the 'map' God has provided. I can turn to the Bible and find guidance and help. This is a map and guide which leads unerringly through precipitous territory.

> **❝**All Scripture is God-breathed and is useful for teaching,
> rebuking, correcting and training in righteousness, so that
> the man of God may be thoroughly equipped for every
> good work. **❞**
> FROM PAUL'S SECOND LETTER TO TIMOTHY, CHAPTER 3.

Gentians were the favourite flower of the
friend who made it possible for me to
become a florist. Arrange them simply, in a
pin-holder covered with moss.

Magnolia

Behind partially closed curtains in my hospital ward was an elderly woman named Annie — I have never seen anyone so crippled and twisted with arthritis. Her joints stood out grotesquely, all over her body, and the slightest movement gave her great pain. Yet I never heard her complain, although washing and bedmaking were agony for her. She was tender and caring towards the nurses throughout their ministrations.

Sometimes I was wheeled to her bedside to talk to her and she was always encouraging in her desire to see me walk again. Being then a selfish sixteen-year-old, I lost touch with her when she left hospital, and I have no idea what happened to her. But whenever I see a magnolia — old, gnarled and twisted — putting forth its fragrant, perfect waxen blossoms, I am reminded of Annie.

Jesus thought and prayed for others, even as the soldiers hammered nails into his hands and he hung on the cross in agony. Only the sustaining strength and love of God himself can enable us to cope with our pain and suffering without bitterness.

> **"** O Lord, do not forsake me; be not far from me, O my God.
> Come quickly to help me, O Lord my Saviour. **"**
> FROM PSALM 38

Cut the magnolia, carefully avoiding touching the blooms, split the ends and stand in deep water overnight. Arrange the blooms in a pin-holder in a shallow dish. Cover the holder with moss, pebbles and leaves.

Honeysuckle

On warm May evenings in late spring, the perfume of the honeysuckle scents the air: the delicate pink-veined flower-buds open and spread their trumpets in the sunshine. Our honeysuckle clambers up a drainpipe and telephone wire. It looks a terrible mess in the winter, but suddenly the mass of scrawny, dead-looking stems bursts into a haze of green, pink and cream.

It always seems extraordinary to me that something that appears so dead can produce such a fragrant flower. It just shows that it does not do to judge by appearances.

People, like the honeysuckle, can seem dead, brittle and hard. I have met many women like that, maybe because they are hurting inside. I can be like it myself. But God's love warms and reaches into the very depths of our being, touching and transforming our cramped spirits, until once again there is a surge of new life.

Whenever we feel 'dead' inside and unable to tell others, we can talk to God about it and ask for his help. And we can look for the answer! It may be a long wintry wait, but it will come as surely as the flower in the wood — the honeysuckle.

> **❝**The Lord is close to the brokenhearted and saves those who are crushed in spirit. **❞**
> FROM PSALM 34

Cut honeysuckle in bud, crush the wooden stems, and place in deep water.

Bluebells

Is there anything more beautiful than a bluebell wood? The swathes of blue and the elusive perfume cannot fail to touch the senses. The soft green beech leaves soar above, allowing the sun to high-light every delicate bell. If we look closely, we can sometimes find a white bluebell hiding among the blue and hidden by fronds of young, curly bracken.

There is a small copse full of bluebells near our house, and each year I inspect every stage of development, from the appearance of the tiny green shaft at the base of the leaves until the drooping full-bodied flowers are finished.

It is one of my favourite places to walk and pray. Many problems have been shared with God, and praises given, among the bluebells. Do those in our lane who walk their dogs in the wood go there to pray, too, I wonder? I know that some do so. But the bluebells keep their own counsel — and our secrets — in that marvellous place of tranquillity and peace. Jesus tells us to pray in secret, shutting the door behind us. But I'm sure he understands why I really do prefer the bluebell wood in spring.

> **❝** Do not be anxious about anything, but in everything, by prayer and petition, with thanksgiving, present your requests to God. **❞**
>
> FROM PAUL'S LETTER TO THE PHILIPPIANS, CHAPTER 4

Place bluebells in warm water overnight to reduce shock, then mass in a deep, water-filled pottery container.

Phlox

Two colourful prints hang on our dining-room wall; the artist obviously loved cottage gardens, and both pictures depict cobbled paths and thatched roofs. Nasturtiums, hollyhocks, delphiniums, roses and tree-mallow, rudbeckia, phlox and irises bloom in an everlasting summer along the paths, in complete contrast to the thick snow just now outside our windows. It is the coldest winter for years and our garden phlox and delphiniums lie dormant in the dark earth wrapped in a white blanket as they wait for the thaw and the sun's warmth to start them into growth.

Our painted cottage flowers are never attacked by mould, greenfly or black spot. I wish I could say the same for the garden ones. But at least my phlox are real. Their slightly acrid scent and soft petals make a colourful show, and we appreciate their reality during the season.

It is enticing to live in a pretend world of perpetual summer, to shut our eyes to the real world about us. But life is not perfect and never will be until Jesus comes again. In the meantime he expects us to grasp reality and deal with it.

I enjoy looking at my pictures, but it is time to put on my boots and start shovelling snow!

66 As the soil makes the sprout come up and a garden causes seeds to grow, so the Sovereign Lord will make righteousness and praise spring up before all nations. 99
FROM ISAIAH CHAPTER 61

Use cottage flowers—phlox, rosemary, roses, delphinium—and recreate a garden border in a large bowl.

Violets

My mother was one of a large family and every spring all the children were herded together to go violetting across the hills. It was the first outing of the year and they would frolic and scramble up the chalky screes to the woods above, hunting out the modest, perfumed violet. Tired but happy, they returned home clutching bunches of flowers tied with wool.

When my mother and father began courting, their first walk together took them to the familiar hills in search of this tiny, exquisite flower and, for the rest of their married life, father presented mother with a nosegay of violets on the anniversary of their first walk together.

Such a little, unobtrusive flower, the violet nestles under its leaves. Searching for the purple heads is like taking part in a treasure hunt.

It is remarkably easy in life to forget the little things that can mean so much — the warm embrace, the timely letter, the unexpected phone-call, or sympathetic ear. Violets increase through being picked, and the small gestures of love start ripples which may have a greater impact than we can ever imagine.

> 66 Dear children, let us not love with words or
> tongue but with actions and in truth. 99
> FROM THE FIRST LETTER OF IOHN, CHAPTER 3

Arrange violets in half an eggshell, with a few leaves.

Meadow Grass

I believe God has a great sense of humour! Who but God would choose an ordinary woman with one useless arm to arrange flowers in front of hundreds of people and share with them the good news about him? God is constantly telling us, in every way possible, that our weakness is his strength and that he loves and uses imperfect, insignificant people to spread the word of his forgiveness and love.

In the natural world, meadow grass is of immense value to all the creatures that depend on it. It gives them sustenance and life. Here, too, God uses ordinary, insignificant elements of his creation to play a vital, life-giving role.

When I first became a Christian, all the world seemed rosy. The love and presence of Jesus carried me through the minor problems of daily living. Then one day the thing I had often dreaded happened. I lost the use of my good hand and arm. It was only for a few weeks but I was really helpless.

During the time of enforced and undesired rest, God used my weakness to teach me more of him. I learned to talk to him in prayer and he talked to me through relevant passages in the Bible. It was a period of spiritual growth for which I shall always be grateful.

> **66** My grace is sufficient for you, for my power is made perfect in weakness. **99**
>
> FROM PAUL'S SECOND LETTER TO THE CORINTHIANS, CHAPTER 12.

Simple meadow grasses, arranged in a household container, add delight to any corner of the room.

Lilies

There is a beautiful bay in Turkey: the brilliant blue sea is surrounded by pine-clad hills; an ancient white fortress juts out from the harbour wall. The hillsides and valleys shelter time-locked villages, where the women sit cross-legged on mats sorting their hard-won produce. In the sand dunes below lie a tumble of ancient stones. The air breathes a sense of past generations and history.

White lilies grow in the sand to the sea's edge and hundreds of small white snails make their home among the stems.

One night, after a violent storm, the sea swept in assorted debris and litter — plastic bags, bottles and dozens of shoes covered the beach. It was a disgusting sight. Some of the lilies continued to bloom pathetically above plastic-wrapped stems.

It is heart-breaking the way we humans spoil our planet. We spoil our minds too, by filling them with rubbish and allowing ourselves to be entertained by violence and pornography.

The unforgettable sight of those beautiful white lilies is a constant personal reminder to care for God's world, and to fill my mind with things that are wholesome and good.

> 66 Whatever is true, whatever is noble, whatever is right, whatever is pure, whatever is lovely, whatever is admirable — if anything is excellent or praiseworthy — think about such things. 99
>
> FROM PAUL'S LETTER TO THE PHILIPPIANS, CHAPTER 4

Orange enchantment lilies are arranged with blackened branches in a black stand.

Wallflowers

When I was a little girl — a long time ago — I used to visit an aunt who possessed a magnificent oil painting of wallflowers in a bowl. When I stood on tiptoe, right in front of it, all I could see was a mass of colour. But, standing back, the design of the rich, velvety wallflowers sprang into focus.

This lovely painting made a deep impression on me and, when we established our first home, I was thrilled to find wallflower-printed furnishing fabric, now alas scuffed into oblivion by the children's sandals and wriggling bottoms!

Wallflowers have a habit of seeding themselves in any odd crack or pocket of soil. From apparently hostile surroundings — the top of a dry stone wall, or between paving stones — they send forth fragrance.

I learned a lesson from the wallflower picture, quite apart from its beauty. If I step back and look at our chaotic and confusing world, through God's eyes, it is possible even now to see something of the beauty he originally intended and which he will one day restore.

> 66 God saw all that he had made, and it was very good. 99
> FROM GENESIS, CHAPTER 1

> 66 Our present sufferings are not worth comparing with the glory that will be revealed in us...Creation itself will be liberated from its bondage to decay. 99
> FROM PAUL'S LETTER TO THE ROMANS, CHAPTER 8

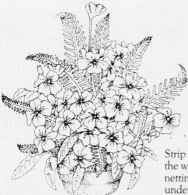

Strip all the lower leaves from the stems of the wallflowers and arrange them in wire netting, completely covering the bowl underneath.

Fuchsias

There is one particular flower I find fascinating: the fuchsia. My husband has just discovered the many different varieties available and is busy taking cuttings, potting and re-potting, even though the flower borders are crying for attention! He brings me the fuchsia-heads and we examine and exclaim over the varying shapes and shades of the blossoms.

There are ballerina frills and slinky skirts, long sinewy petals and short perky ones. It is amazing that one flower family can produce such incredibly different shapes and colours. I cannot bear to see the flower-heads left to die, so I pop them on a saucer in the kitchen, enjoying them as I admire the parent-plants through the window.

The Christian family is like the fuchsia family in its infinite variety. It is a wide family of different nations, different cultures — all united because we belong to Jesus. God does not force us into one mould. He delights in variety — every person different and special. Each bringing something unique to the whole family.

> **66** Accept one another, then, just as Christ accepted you, in order to bring praise to God. **99**
> FROM PAUL'S LETTER TO THE ROMANS, CHAPTER 15

Arrange fuchias in a tall oasis-filled container, allowing their graceful stems to curve and display their blossoms.

Carnations

M any years ago my small brother sat on the ground, turning out the contents of his pockets. Among the sticky sweets and string he unearthed a few pence and, after disappearing into the nearby florist's, he emerged beaming, clutching three carnations which he proudly presented to our mother. She was quite over-whelmed by the richness of this gift from her small son.

Recently history repeated itself. Another little boy — my nephew — tired from a long aeroplane flight, gave three silk flowers from his new brother and himself to the grandmother they had never seen before. What a loving introduction. And as the children return home the little silk flowers will remain to remind their grandmother of the strands of love spanning the distance.

God our Father opens his arms to welcome new members into his family. He asks us, not for gifts or flowers, but to give ourselves, trusting him to receive us. Jesus has left us a remembrance and a promise of reunion with him. As we taste the wine and eat the bread at the communion service our hearts warm to the knowledge of the depth and breadth of God's love and concern for us all.

> 66 And he took bread, gave thanks and broke it, and gave it to them, saying, 'This is my body given for you; do this in remembrance of me.' 99
>
> FROM LUKE'S GOSPEL, CHAPTER 22

Three carnations are arranged at different heights, using their own foilage, in a green glass bottle.

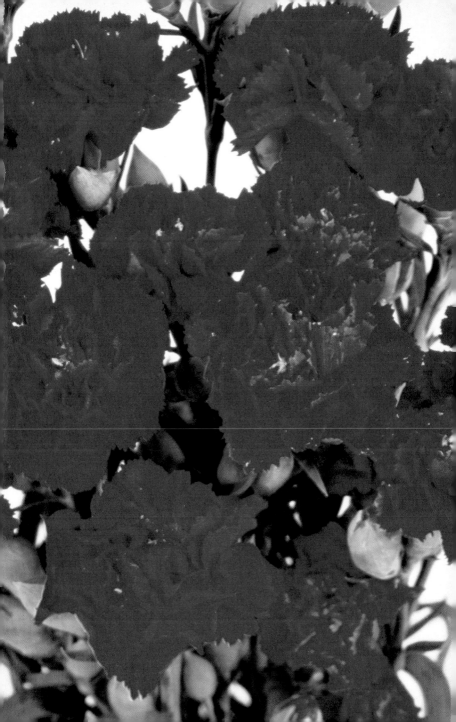

Heart's-ease Pansies

Tiny flowers with miniature faces, heart's-ease pansies grow close to the ground. Their purple, yellow and white blooms look up, waiting to be recognized and acknowledged. Left to themselves they flourish and grow into large families, ignoring their more flamboyant cultivated sisters.

My grandmother loved pansies; the heart's-ease was her favourite. She said they looked so cheerful, whatever the weather — a lesson for us, perhaps.

In Victorian flower arranging, the pansy meant 'thoughts'. I have a very old book on the meaning of flowers, which explains how we can flatter, care, send messages, or even insult someone by choosing the appropriate flower. A shy young man could send his beloved a bunch of red and white clover, meaning 'Think of me and be mine.' The heart's-ease, by its name, reminds us to become channels through which God can show love and compassion to those whose minds are ill-at-ease. Jesus spent his time on earth ministering to multitudes who followed him day and night, easing pain and lifting burdens. Following his example, we can be a heart's-ease to one another.

> **66** When Jesus saw the crowds, he had compassion on them, because they were harrassed and helpless, like sheep without a shepherd. **99**
> FROM MATTHEW'S GOSPEL, CHAPTER 9

Arrange heart's-ease pansies in a small pot inside a miniature basket, tie a ribbon bow over the handle and give as a gift.

Heather

You really have to get down on your knees to study the tiny flowers of the low-growing Erica family, yet each one contributes to the overall effect of a purple or white spray. When the heather is out, the hills are a blaze of colour. In the garden there are enough varieties of heather to give colour all the year round. A tiny sprig or two adds charm to any small arrangement.

Heather, for me, brings back a visit we made to a group of young people, all badly disabled. Some were unable to speak, walk or move. I thought then of the heather bells so quiet, individually apparently insignificant, yet enriching all our lives. These young men and women all loved Jesus. There was joy on their faces as we spoke of him. Although some were stunted in growth, their spiritual life was full-bodied and strong, influencing all who came in contact with them.

It is tempting to write off as useless all that is not perfect. But how wrong we are. Not all the heather bells are perfect but, integrated with others, they bring beauty into our lives. And these disabled brothers and sisters of mine enriched my perception of God's blessing.

66 God chose the foolish things of the world to shame the wise; God chose the weak things of the world to shame the strong. He chose the lowly things of this world and the despised things ... so that no one may boast before him. **99**

FROM PAUL'S FIRST LETTER TO THE CORINTHIANS, CHAPTER 1

Arrange sprigs of heather and tiny
rosebuds in a small clean plastic container,
to give as a gift.

Rosehips and Wild Clematis

The sweet fresh scents and the low autumnal sunshine illuminate a new aspect of the natural world about us. Plant stems and leaves throw long shadows and flower-heads glisten with silvery dew. The leaves of maple and beech shiver and float gently to the ground, settling into a patterned carpet before they dry and crisp beneath our feet. Jewelled necklaces of berries tangle with the spiral-headed clematis, as it begins to burst into fluffy white seedheads.

When does our own 'autumn' begin? My first white hairs came in my twenties! It may be the aches and pains of a damp morning, or a realization that our energy levels are not as high as they were, which alert us to the passing years.

But the autumnal world of plant and human life has its own beauty. And in the case of people, one of the benefits should be a greater understanding of human nature. There is still a positive role for the older ones among us. We all need the wisdom and illumination which they can provide.

> **66** Even when I am old and grey, do not forsake me, O God, till I declare your power to the next generation, your might to all who are to come. **99**
> FROM PSALM 71

Fill a rough pottery container with rosehips and wild clematis, spraying the fluffy heads with hair lacquer to prevent them shedding hairs!

Dahlias

A wedding brings great changes into a family — in our own case, a son given but a charming daughter gained. As we stood in the dahlia-decorated church, I reflected over the years that had passed so quickly. A tiny baby, a rampaging toddler, long-haired teenager and now a fully responsible young man beginning a new way of life.

For me that special day will always be linked with dahlias. A fragile head of petals held on a sturdy stem encourages me to think that although marriage too has its difficult, fragile moments there can be real strength in a relationship and commitment to one another which depends on mutual unselfishness and a growing trust in God.

As September — the anniversary — approaches once again, a big bunch of dahlias will arrive on our son's doorstep — a small reminder to them both of a happy day and our prayers for their future and continuing love and happiness together.

66 At the beginning of creation God 'made them male and female.' 'For this reason a man will leave his father and mother and be united to his wife, and the two will become one flesh.' So they are no longer two, but one. Therefore what God has joined together, let man not separate. 99
FROM MARK'S GOSPEL, CHAPTER 10

Arrange dahlias in a tin-lined basket, using foliage to soften the severity of their stems.

Holly

Those of us who live in western Europe associate holly with Christmas decorations. The dark green, shiny leaves and lipstick-red berries start beckoning my attention from October or November onwards. Then it is a race to see which gets there first — the birds or my eager hands. I usually forget to wear gloves, and the barbed leaves prickle and hurt, however gingerly they are carried. But the swathes and garlands for the home adequately compensate for the wounds inflicted!

Many of us tend to be prickly too. All too often we hurt one another. Misunderstandings and thoughtlessness can really get under our skins, not to mention the barbed remarks from our unruly tongues. I could often bite mine off — wishing things unsaid!

Christmas is a good time to remember God's message of peace and goodwill to all humankind. With his help our lives can bear the fruit of love, patience and self-control, as berries on the holly bough.

> 66 We love because he first loved us. If anyone says, 'I love God,' yet hates his brother, he is a liar. For anyone who does not love his brother, whom he has seen, cannot love God, whom he has not seen. And he has given us this command: Whoever loves God must also love his brother. 99
>
> FROM THE FIRST LETTER OF JOHN, CHAPTER 4

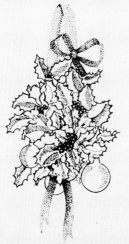

Place a soaked oasis ball in a plastic bag, and cover with short-stemmed holly, wired baubles and bright hanging ribbons.

Gerbera

I have a special reason for choosing the gerbera to close this book. The gerbera, surrounded by lilies of the valley, was the centre-piece of my bridal bouquet. So it is a way of saying thank you to my husband for his love, support and patience during the writing of these pages. After a hard day's work, he has sifted, advised and reminded me of different events we have shared together. This is very much a family book: our daughter typed the pages and our sons regularly enquired about its progress, making helpful if outlandish suggestions! I thank God for all this love and support.

As a family, we have loved and grown together through crises and joys and during all these years we have been surrounded by God's love and faithfulness. God loves us all, not just as individuals, but as families, too, and he brings everyone who loves him into his worldwide family. When we give our lives and loyalty to Jesus we enter into the Christian family, with God as our Father.

So now to you who have shared in my memories of family and home, I offer these flowers — with love.

> **66** Bear with each other and forgive whatever grievances you may have against one another. Forgive as the Lord forgives you. And over all these virtues put on love, which binds them all together in perfect unity. **99**
>
> FROM PAUL'S LETTER TO THE COLOSSIANS, CHAPTER 3

One single gerbera, impaled on a pin-holder surrounded by pieces of twisted wood, is dramatic and unusual.